HOW TO
FURNITURE

An Easy Reference Guide

TREVOR YORKE

COUNTRYSIDE BOOKS
NEWBURY BERKSHIRE

COUNTRYSIDE BOOKS
3 Catherine Road
Newbury, Berkshire

To view our complete range of books
please visit us at
www.countrysidebooks.co.uk

ISBN 978 1 84674 376 4

Illustrations by the author

All materials used in the manufacture of this book carry FSC certification

Produced by The Letterworks Ltd., Reading
Typeset by KT Designs, St Helens
Printed by The Holywell Press, Oxford

CONTENTS

INTRODUCTION

Antique furniture is more than a functional item adorned with fancy woodwork. It can be a work of art with intricate inlaid strips, elaborate patterned marquetry and vigorous carving which display a cabinet maker's skill. The shape and size of a piece can record changes in social habits and the introduction of new fashions from the continent or further afield. The richness of its decoration and fittings can reflect the ambitions and wealth of the person who commissioned or bought it. Old furniture can also be full of surprises with secret compartments, mysterious locks and clever mechanisms, which can turn a mundane-looking piece into a glorious treasure trove. Even the material it is made from and the way it was finished record the opening up of new trade routes and methods of manufacturing.

With so many changes in the form, function and style of furniture from 1500 up to 1900, the range of pieces you can find in old country houses, museums and antique shops can be bewildering to the novice. If you add to this the numerous cabinet makers who are referred to, a technical terminology which is often unfamiliar, and the problem with recognising original work from Victorian and modern reproductions, then the confusion in compounded.

This illustrated book has been created to help the beginner through this minefield and enjoy the thrill of being able to recognise the style and approximately date old pieces of furniture. There is a detailed Glossary of Terms on page 62.

The book begins with a brief journey through the history of English furniture and introduces the key styles. Each chapter looks at specific pieces, from tables and chairs to cabinets and chests, and arranges them chronologically to make it easier to recognise the changes in form and decoration. The book is packed with my own drawings, most of which were specifically produced for this book, along with captions which point out the key details to help narrow down the date when a piece was made. Finally there is a short piece to help you identify fakes from the genuine article.

Whether you are looking to learn about antiques, to choose appropriate pieces for a period home or you would just like to enhance your visit to a National Trust property, this book will be a useful introduction to an ever fascinating subject.

Trevor Yorke

Follow me on Facebook at
trevoryorke-author
Or visit my website:
www.trevoryorke.co.uk

4

ENGLISH FURNITURE

A brief history

Furniture has always been the focal point of a home, no matter who lives there. The oldest house in Northern Europe with standing walls, at Knap of Howar on the Orkney Islands, still has the remains of stone cupboards within, despite being over 5,000 years old. Our grandest country houses would be hollow shells were in not for elaborate pieces of furniture which speak volumes about the ambitions of their wealthy owners. Even the most modern houses, viewed on television design shows, are only brought to life by the clever use of materials and the artistic form of tables, sofas and kitchen units.

Old furniture is more than just a nostalgic antique; the finest pieces are artistic creations displaying the craftsman's skill and designer's flair. They can reflect the social status and functional requirements of the person who bought it. For instance luxurious and decorative pieces designed for play or display could only be afforded by a family of means who had the spare time to use them, or someone with the ambitions to be a member of that class. Their form and function can also record changes in society. Bookcases were of no use to most Tudor families when they received a largely practical education, but were an essential item for an 18th-century gentleman who wanted to display beautifully bound books to reflect a learned background. The material from which each piece is made has been determined by the availability of a particular wood and the changes in fashion. A harsh winter across Europe in 1709 wiped out most walnut trees which was then the favoured wood for luxurious furniture to the extent that the French banned its export in 1720. However, in the following year the lifting of duty on the import of mahogany from the Caribbean islands would help make this exotic new timber walnut's fashionable replacement.

Global events, like major wars or political disputes, also affected the design of furniture. Henry VIII's fall-out with the Pope resulted in Britain being cut off from the main flow of continental fashions for much of the 16th century, and so domestic furniture from this period can appear old fashioned in form. Conversely, the ending of Puritan rule and the Restoration to the throne in 1660 of Charles II, who had spent his exile lapping up the latest in French and Dutch fashions, helped ignite a period of rapid development and change in English furniture. The style of pieces was also determined by location. Leading manufacturers in London supplying cosmopolitan homes had to encompass the latest trends here and in Europe, new designs which would take time to filter out to provincial towns. In more remote parts of the country, traditional forms could last on for centuries and pieces were created which were unique to a local area.

For a fuller knowledge about those who made or originally bought early furniture, it is essential to recognise and understand when the pieces were made. The expert with a lifetime of knowledge can amaze us with their ability to date furniture, but there are general trends in the form, function, material and decoration of pieces which can help those new to the subject narrow down the period from which it came. Before looking at the different types of furniture in the following chapters it is worth spending a brief moment looking at the general changes in style over the last 500 years which have affected their design.

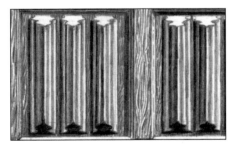

FIG 1.1: Linenfold panelling (top) is distinctive of the early Tudor period. Strapwork patterns (bottom, left-hand side) were popular in the late 16th and early 17th centuries.

FURNITURE STYLES

Style and fashion were not of great interest to most medieval lords. Their homes were judged more on their grandeur, facilities and the size of their household rather than the design of their interiors. Their great halls and private chambers would have been colourful places and often richly decorated, but furniture was limited and generally functional. During the 15th century, the Renaissance, the rebirth of art and architecture from the Ancient world, inspired a new approach to design with a focus on symmetry, proportions and the use of the Classical orders. In the 1530s, just as these new ideas permeated into British culture, Henry VIII made his fateful break from Rome and for over a century the country was cast adrift from the main flow of continental fashions. Designers only had second hand knowledge of the latest Classical styles and so applied columns, round arches and motifs to traditional forms without a clear understanding of how they were meant to be used. Despite this cultural isolation, the wealth of the nation was growing and a new generation of merchants and yeoman farmers began to demand some of the luxuries previously reserved for nobles. This helped create a demand for new pieces of furniture in oak, which would not only provide greater comfort and convenience but could also reflect their new found status.

The Restoration of the monarchy in 1660 meant that Charles II, who had spent much of his exile in France and the Low Countries, brought back with him a desire for their fashions and the craftsmen who could execute them. It coincided too with the pent-up demand for worldly and stylish goods from a public that had been denied them during the austerity of the Civil War as well as in Cromwell's subsequent joyless rule. When William of Orange was invited to take the throne in 1688 he too inspired a new passion this time for all things Dutch. Foreign trade was booming and imports of desirable luxury items, like Chinese porcelain and lacquered cabinets, began to arrive from the Far East. The late 17th century was also a period of religious persecution in France which resulted in Protestants, known as Huguenots, fleeing and settling in Britain. They came in large numbers and many were skilled craftsmen who introduced new methods of manufacturing furniture and upholstery. Veneered walnut replaced solid oak as the timber of choice and the latter tended to be restricted to rural areas for more traditional types of furniture.

FIG 1.2: An example *of the rich and exuberant Baroque style carving perfected by Grinling Gibbons in the late 17th century. This talented English carver was the finest exponent of the art and much of his best work was for the royal family.*

The heavy, box-shaped pieces with deep carving which were associated with earlier work began to be superseded by finer, less solid types. The finest could have marquetry patterns over the whole surface, intricate carving inspired by the work of Grinling Gibbons, and busy turned legs with bold scrolls.

Classical styles dominated the design of interiors during the first half of the 18th century from the Baroque with its grandeur and exuberant features to the more refined and elegant Palladian. The reign of Queen Anne, whose name is closely associated with furniture designed in the first two decades of the century, is marked by more curvaceous forms which had developed since the 1690s, and more restrained decoration. The Cabriole leg, named after the Italian word for 'goat's leap' due to it resembling a goat's lower leg, was introduced around the turn of the new century. By the 1720s, mahogany began to replace walnut as the timber of choice for high-class furniture. Marquetry fell from fashion and decoration became heavier, grand and more architectural in form on many pieces of furniture. William Kent was the leading designer of the age and created pieces with heavy carved Classical features, foliage and masks often completely covered in gilt.

Furniture in the middle of the 18th century was shaped by a more rapidly changing palette of styles which were manipulated by a new breed of highly skilled designers and craftsmen based in London. The Rococo inspired richly ornate furniture with asymmetrical forms, fluid curves, and shell or rock elements often finished in white paint and gilt. At the same time as this French style became popular, so other pieces were influenced by the decoration on imported Chinese products, with geometric fretwork patterns and pagoda shaped roofs being a distinctive feature. Even the Gothic, which had long been viewed as barbaric and outdated, was re-imagined by Batty Langley and Horace Walpole, usually with pointed arches and medieval decoration added onto symmetrical Classical forms. As a growing number of smart new urban developments and grand country houses were being erected so new furniture designers and companies were established to supply them with an increasingly wide range of furniture types and styles. The most famous of these was Thomas Chippendale, a designer and manufacturer whose *The Gentleman and Cabinet-Maker's Director*, first published in 1754,

FIG 1.3: Many rooms were still multifunctional *in the early Georgian period so furniture had to be moved up against the wall at certain times. Tables, for instance, had flaps which could be dropped so this could be easily done. Dado rails were also fitted on walls, as in this view of a drawing room, to prevent the wall coverings being damaged by chairs and tables.*

included drawings of his elegantly proportioned and stylish new forms of furniture which influenced a generation of craftsmen. Ince and Mayhew, Robert Mainwaring and Sir William Chambers were other manufacturers and designers working in this period.

Up to this point, Classical styles had been largely based upon the work of Renaissance architects and their interpretation of a limited number of Roman ruins. From the 1750s, new discoveries and detailed studies of the ruins from the wider Ancient world, introduced a new range of forms and motifs. Robert Adam used these to create a distinctive Neoclassical style in which he designed every aspect of the house interior including the furniture and fittings. These were distinguished by delicate, shallow patterns on a white or pastel-coloured background with round medallions, urns, mythological beasts and fine swags of husks or bell flowers. Satinwood began to displace mahogany as the most fashionable wood; marquetry was revived and then in turn was superseded by painted finishes with colourful floral motifs or gilt decoration.

The French Revolution and Napoleonic Wars and the limits this imposed on continental travel helped focus British

FIG 1.4: Motifs used by Robert Adam. *Honeysuckle (left), Patera (centre left), a medallion (centre right) and husks (right).*

eyes more closely on their own historic past and inspired a fresh interest in the Gothic. At first this was still applied in a rather whimsical manner with some interiors drowned in a sea of pointed arches and pinnacles, but by the 1830s it was becoming a more serious and sombre style. Despite conflict with France the new Empire style proved influential on this side of the Channel. It embraced the Classical glories of Ancient Rome, Greece and Egypt, and had strong forms with lavish gilt or bronze fittings.

As trading routes around the globe expanded so a taste for the exotic developed, most extravagantly seen in The Prince Regent's Royal Pavilion in Brighton, whilst the more restrained Neoclassical style and austere Greek Revival also influenced furniture design. This Regency period is also notable for the acceptance of sham materials. Cheaper softwoods could be stained or grained to appear as a

FIG 1.5: By the Regency period *most furniture was now left in place within the room so there was less need to make them portable. The fashion for lounging and relaxing made comfortable chairs, sofas and the chaise lounge popular as in this example of a drawing room.*

finer quality timber, or the whole piece could be painted so that materials like papier-mâché and mass produced resin mouldings could be used. The most influential book during this period was Thomas Sheraton's *The Cabinet-Maker and Upholsterer's Drawing-Book* which popularised slender, elegant and rectangular forms of furniture with straight legs and Neoclassical detailing.

By the mid-19th century the expanding middle classes were demanding the trappings of their superiors on a broader scale. For the first time, the acquisition of opulent fixtures and fittings through a second-hand market became acceptable. Reproduction furniture became widely available and was designed to satisfy their desire for luxurious furnishings in a chosen historic style rather than for its elegance or inventiveness. This ranged from Elizabethan, Grecian, and Louis XVI styles early in the Victorian period to a revival of interest in Chippendale and Sheraton later in the century. A.W.N. Pugin inspired a new Gothic Revival based upon accurate studies of medieval forms and pointed arches, with patterns of tracery and richly carved foliage adorning the sometimes heavy and severe oak furniture pieces created during the 1850s and 60s. In the following decades there was a reaction against this sea of mass-produced, eclectic styles and a new generation of designers introduced simplified forms. Japan began to open up to foreign trade and its distinctive style of furniture with ebonised surfaces, rectilinear (straight line) fretwork, and stylised landscapes was the height of fashion in the 1870s.

The Arts and Crafts movement idealised the medieval period as a time of honest craftsmanship and those working under its banner revived traditional methods of construction and materials while creating refreshing, simple pieces of furniture with intricate handmade iron and brass fittings. Charles Rennie Mackintosh admired Japanese design and created a unique style, blending elegant rectilinear forms with stylised floral motifs. This was influential on the continent where Art Nouveau, with its sinuous foliage, flowers and figurines, was fashionable in the first decade of the 20th century. After the First World War, exotic pieces inspired by African art and the discovery of Tutankhamun's tomb inspired a new brand of exotic furniture, although reproductions of 18th-century pieces still remained very popular. However, by the 1930s the modernist movement, which sought to create furniture that used the advantages of machine production whilst avoiding unnecessary decoration, began to gain in influence. Its radical, efficient and sometimes ingenious designs in plywood, chromium and Bakelite might have been too modern for most British homes but would be more readily accepted by a younger audience after the Second World War.

French Influence

France has long been at the forefront of fashionable furniture design. Its influence on English furniture was most notable from the mid-17th century through to the end of the 18th century when the French and English courts were periodically in close contact and immigrants fleeing France introduced their latest styles and techniques here. This period coincided with the reigns of Louis XIV (14th), XV (15th) and XVI (16th) and the changing styles are usually referred to by the monarch.

Louis XIV who reigned from 1643-1715 created a court of extravagant magnificence centred upon his Palace of Versailles. Furniture reflected the fashionable Baroque style with bold, large-scale features and rich, formal decoration with gilded scrollwork, intricate patterned surfaces and marble tops. The fashion for all-over marquetry and scrolled legs was particularly influential in England.

During the reign of Louis XV from 1715-1774 interiors became more intimate and furniture became less massive to suit. The Rococo style developed unrestrained by strict Classical rules so the new pieces could have a serpentine, bulbous shape with asymmetrical decoration overwhelmed by lively foliage, shells and encrusted carving in gold, white and pastel colours. Although this style was too extreme for many English patrons, it inspired Thomas Chippendale in the shape of some of his cabinets and commodes and details on chairs and tables.

By the time Louis XVI came to the throne in 1774 styles had begun to shift away from curves and florid decoration to the straight lines and restrained Classical motifs of the Neoclassical style. Pieces became lighter and graceful with thin tapered legs, metal mounts and oval and half-moon shapes, often with a light coloured, painted finish featuring flowers, ribbons and rustic motifs. This last flowering before the king was ousted during the French Revolution in 1793 has close parallels with the work of Robert Adam and inspired many designers in England including the graceful curves of some of George Hepplewhite's designs and Thomas Sheraton's love of painted furniture.

CHAIRS

Dining chairs, armchairs, sofas and settees

Chairs are perhaps the most important part of one's furniture, not only for their practical advantages but also because their form frequently changed as an expression of the latest fashion and provided increasing levels of comfort. The shape of the back, the types of leg, the style of the upholstery, and the timber used add great variety to those which can be seen in country houses and antique shops.

Despite being taken for granted today, chairs did not become an everyday item in most households until around 300 years ago. Even in the homes of the wealthy they were a rare sight until the early 17th century as most people of all classes used benches and stools. The word chair is derived from the Latin 'cathedra', as in cathedral, the seat of a bishop, which highlights its original high status for the head of the household.

Early seats were solid and boxy until the second half of the 17th century, when more open and elegant designs began to evolve. Comfort was not a top priority, a cushion might be provided for some relief until upholstered chairs became common in the early 18th century. During the Georgian period new types were introduced including hall chairs, dining chairs, armchairs, writing chairs, settees, sofas and chaises longues which individually catered for different social activities or were designed to suit specific rooms. Away from the finest homes provincial pieces in oak, or a cheap wood which was painted or grained, were produced, including the versatile Windsor chair. The Victorians focused more on comfort and luxury with historic association rather than inventive style but towards the end of the period simplified forms with restrained decoration gained a niche market.

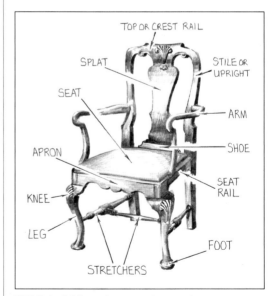

FIG 2.1: A Victorian *reproduction dining chair with labels of the key parts.*

11

FIG 2.3: Late medieval and early Tudor
*chairs had a square form with solid sides
and back (left) and were often referred to as
wainscot (wooden panelling) chairs.
By the second half of the 16th century open
sides became common and later Jacobean
types had turned front legs with arm
uprights in line and richly carved back panels
(right). This form remained popular in
many regions throughout the 17th century.
Stretchers in these periods were linked
on all four sides and set close to the ground
so the seated person could rest their
feet upon them to keep out of the dirty
rushes and straw which covered the
floor.*

FIG 2.2: Joyn'd or joint stools *were the
most common form of seating in the 16th and
17th centuries. Early types had solid ends but
by the Jacobean period they usually had four
turned (see glossary) legs linked by stretchers
with varying degrees of decoration, as in this
example. The parts were fixed by mortise and
tenon (see glossary) joints held in place by
wooden pegs. Their height varied from those
around 550mm for sitting at a table, 450mm
for general use and 300-400mm which were
footstools or for children. With a flat top they
could easily be adapted to other uses.*

FIG 2.4: Settles are a distinctive form *of
large seat from the Tudor and Jacobean period.
Some were open underneath but many had this
area panelled off and used for storage. A few
even had a hinged back panel which could tilt
over to turn the settle into a table. 17th century
examples tend to have numerous plain panels
with carving and moulding around the frame as in
this example, a favourite form for most Jacobean
seating. Settles continued to be made in rural
areas well into the 18th century and were revived
by the Arts and Crafts movement.*

FIG 2.5: A back stool *was a common form of chair in the first half of the 17th century, which was literally a square framed stool with a back. Fixed upholstery was introduced in this period with this example, commonly referred to as a Cromwellian or Puritan chair, featuring a thick leather cover pinned to the frame by rows of brass headed nails, a popular form during the 1640s and 50s. The style of the turned front legs and stretchers in this example are distinctive of this period although the back legs were usually plain and straight, so leaning back would have been hazardous.*

FIG 2.6: Chairs *in the second half of the 17th century had taller, narrower backs and rear legs which slightly splayed outwards to make them more stable. Walnut was now the timber of choice although oak was still used for provincial chairs. Stretchers were higher off the ground as the finest houses now had floor coverings, and the front one was often arched and carved to match the crest rail along the top of the chair back. By the 1690s stretchers could be fixed in an 'x' shape between the legs with a turned knob at the centre point. Turned legs had more elaborate patterns, while later spiral or barley twist and scroll-shaped legs, as shown in this example, became popular. Caning was introduced for the seat and back of chairs as trade increased with the Far East.*

FIG 2.7: In the early 18th century, *fashionable chairs became more curved and serpentine in form (compare with FIG 2.5). Cabriole (see glossary) legs were popular, at first with stretchers but these were dispensed with when the top knee section was enlarged to make a strong joint, as in this example. The feet on the earliest Queen Anne chairs were simple club, hoof or pad shapes but after 1710 the ball clasped by a claw was introduced on the finest examples. The simple hoop back comes into fashion with a solid vertical splat down the centre, either straight-sided or shaped like a fiddle or vase, with carving or marquetry on the best chairs.*

FIG 2.8: Fully upholstered wing chairs and settees *were developed in the first half of the 18th century. Wings were added onto conventional armchairs to help keep draughts away from the seated person's head. At first they appear as separate additions but by the 1730s they tend to flow as one with the back, and later both features are the same height. Settees had evolved from the earlier settles and like the armchair permitted a large display*

of the latest velvets or damasks (a heavy silk fabric with a scrolling foliage design woven in) or wool needlework with a pattern, landscape or mythological scene (FIG 2.9). Chair back settees with a single-piece seat and a row of two, three or more separate chair backs were also popular in the first half of the 18th century. The example shown here in the Baroque style of William Kent dates from the 1730s with gilt frame, animal heads on the ends of the arms and swags and shell carving beneath (the latter feature was a distinctive motif in this period).

FIG 2.9: By the 1740s the French Rococo style *began to influence chair design in England. Although designs were more restrained than in France they still had asymmetrical forms, busy foliage patterns, scrolls, and shell-shaped motifs, with the pieces often painted white or gilt. The arms on chairs were by this period set further back from the front as in this example.*

FIG 2.10: Mahogany *had replaced walnut as the fashionable timber by the 1730s. Backs were lower than in the late 17th century, cabriole legs with claw and ball feet were fashionable and splats were now wider at the top and had pierced decoration as in this example. The shoe socket was a separate piece at the base of the splat by this period.*

FIG 2.11: Thomas Chippendale's *early chair designs move away from backs with hoops to designs with a straighter cresting, often in the shape of Cupid's bow. The splat becomes more open and intricate in design and more elegant scrolls replace the animal heads on the ends of arms, so his chairs appear lighter than earlier Georgian types. Although this example has cabriole legs, he increasingly used straight ones linked by H-shaped stretchers.*

FIG 2.12: The Chinoiserie style, *from 'chinois' the French for Chinese, was popularised by Chippendale with chairs featuring distinctive geometric patterned fretwork backs, as in this example. His Gothic pieces usually had backs comprising pointed arches or cusped tracery patterns with both styles usually mounted upon straight square legs.*

Thomas Chippendale

Born in Otley, Yorkshire in 1718, Thomas Chippendale was probably trained in part by his carpenter father before he established himself in London at the age of 30. Although designs for furniture had been published before, Chippendale's *The Gentleman and Cabinet-Maker's Director* of 1754 was the first large-scale work and was an immediate success. It contained over 150 designs for contemporary pieces including Rococo, Gothic and Chinese styles and when reprinted in 1762 had some of the latest Neoclassical designs added. As his cabinet making business grew, Chippendale would have had less hands-on involvement but would have created new designs, advised clients on interior decorative schemes and taken commissions from architects like Adam and Chambers, while his workforce of artisans produced the actual furniture. Pieces today which are labelled Chippendale are either surviving items from his workshop or more likely those produced by other companies and craftsmen who used his *Director* for inspiration.

FIG 2.13: Popular designs *from Chippendale's Director included ribbon back chairs (left) which highlighted the great designer's admiration of the Louis XV style and his use of 'C' scrolls, and the ladder back which was widely copied by provincial carpenters (right). Chairs in this mid-Georgian period are also notably shorter than those from the turn of the century, usually just over 3ft high (950mm approx.).*

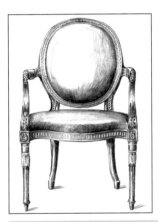

FIG 2.14: Robert Adam style *inspired by new motifs and designs discovered across the Ancient World became the height of fashion in the 1770s and 80s. Although he did not make chairs, the interior schemes he created had pieces commissioned by himself or selected to complement his pastel-shaded and delicately decorated Neoclassical rooms. The fully developed Adam style is distinguished by elegant chairs with a painted or gilt finish featuring shallow carved motifs including strings of bell-like flowers and plain fluted lines as on this example.*

George Hepplewhite

Despite being a household name in furniture the real George Hepplewhite was an elusive character of which very little is known. He is believed to have been a cabinet maker based in London who had around 300 drawings of his designs published by his wife two years after he died in 1786. *The Cabinet-Maker and Upholsterer's Guide* included pieces inspired by Adam with Neoclassical motifs and forms which were popular at the time although many are now associated with Hepplewhite. Shield-shaped backs with a Prince of Wales plume, half wheels at the base of the back, a gap above the seat and straight tapering legs are distinctive of his work. Oval, wheel, saddle and heart-shaped backs and Greek honeysuckle and anthemion (see glossary) motifs were also used.

FIG 2.15: An example of a Hepplewhite chair *with its distinctive shield back.*

FIG 2.16: Upholstered settees and sofas *(probably from the Arabic* suffah *meaning a long upholstered chair) with a serpentine-shaped back and arms scrolled outwards, as in this example, were distinctive of the mid to late 18th century. Bar back sofas were a popular alternative with a row of wooden shield backs and cane seats fitted with loose cushions.*

FIG 2.17: Thomas Sheraton *chairs (right) were lighter and squarer than Hepplewhite's designs. They usually have straight backs which are rectangular in form with a clear gap above the seat, and thin tapering legs which are fluted or reeded with the front supports of the arms an extension of these. Dining room chairs were robust but plain, whereas in the more feminine drawing room his pieces were painted and decorated with motifs including husks, swags, and festoons.*

Thomas Sheraton

Born in Stockton-on-Tees in 1751 and given no academic training, Thomas Sheraton nevertheless became a skilled furniture designer and also an artist, inventor, author and even a Baptist minister in his later life. He spent much of his career as a journeyman cabinet maker until he moved to London when he was nearly 40 and tried to make a living from teaching and consultancy. From 1791 he began publishing *The Cabinet-Maker and Upholsterer's Drawing-Book*, and in 1803 the *Cabinet Dictionary* which was very influential and popularised the new Grecian or Greek Revival style. Sheraton's great skill was as a draughtsman and there are no pieces of furniture positively identified as made by him. He lived above his tiny shop where he sold books. Sadly, he left his wife and two children in poverty when he died in 1806.

FIG 2.18: By the Regency period *painted chairs, which allowed cheaper woods like beech to be used, were very popular. Also in demand were caned or solid wood backs which were horizontally set with the large gap below spanned by a lower support or rail, as in this example.*

FIG 2.19: The Regency period, *which in design terms spans from the 1790s through to the 1830s, witnessed many changes in style from Sheraton-inspired rectilinear pieces through to more curvaceous forms with distinctive sabre-shaped legs. They could be light and delicate in form with a painted finish, especially those for the drawing room, or of a heavier and solid construction in a finely polished wood when destined for the dining room, as in the example here. Rectangular, oval and circular backs were common usually with a horizontal support rail below but vertical splats were now rare. Decoration was more limited in scope than before with carving or brass inlay on back rails, fluting on straight legs and scrolls on arms. Rope moulding and nautical motifs were used to honour the victories of the British Navy while wreaths and fasces (a bundle of rods with an axe head) reflected success during the Napoleonic Wars. Classical-inspired motifs from Ancient Rome, Greece and now Egypt featured on many chairs with gilded animal heads and feet, anthemion, Greek key, and amphorae.*

FIG 2.20: Oval shapes, *cane seats and backs and painted wood were very popular in the Regency period, as in this example. Chinoiserie and gothic styles which had been fashionable in the mid-18th century once again influenced chair design but in a more subtle way with fake bamboo effect on frames or restrained medieval tracery backs. It was acceptable in this period to paint or decorate cheap materials so they appeared to be a finer product.*

FIG 2.21: Excavations by Napoleon's expedition *into Egypt during the 1790s had popularised forms and motifs from this ancient world in addition to those from Greece and Rome. The curule or X-frame chair which was based upon the* sella curulis, *the seat used by Roman senators, was revived. Greek* klismos *chairs, which had four sabre-shaped, outward-curving legs and a concave horizontal back were also to be found. This latter form was adapted into a more conventional form of chair, as in this example, which was popular in this period.*

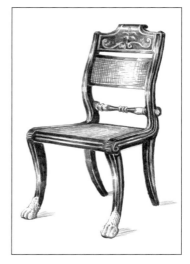

FIG 2.22: A bergère *was typical of the comfortable upholstered seating in the early 19th century, which reflected the fashion for relaxing and lounging in the Regency home. These rectilinear enclosed seats had cushioned backs and seats, often with padding on the arms but had the rest of the framework exposed. They were often made from a softwood which was painted or gilded, or were in hardwood with a waxed finish. There was a wide range of woods used in this period including the fashionable satinwood and rosewood but mahogany, oak and walnut were also favoured for some pieces.*

FIG 2.23: The Grecian sofa *with two scrolled ends and the chaise longue with one, as in this example, were a must-have feature in the finest Regency drawing rooms. Their graceful form featured a scrolled back and cylindrical bolster cushion, sometimes with animal heads and feet on the exposed timber, which is a distinctive feature of early 19th-century furniture.*

FIG 2.24: Early and mid-Victorian chairs *were available in a wide range of woods and styles, with heavier curvaceous frames replacing the rectilinear forms of the early Regency. Balloon-shaped backs are very distinctive of the age as in these examples. Chairs for the drawing room often feature a serpentine front seat rail with the moulding on the corners continuing down the cabriole leg (left). Dining room chairs would usually have straight turned legs and seat rail (right).*

FIG 2.25: Buttoned back upholstered chairs and sofas *were contoured to satisfy the demand for comfort. Sprung seats became fashionable after coil springs were introduced in 1828 with leather, tapestries and other heavy fabrics held by buttons and fixed around the edges popular by the 1850s. Spoon-shaped backs were fashionable on upholstered chairs and those without arms were convenient for ladies wearing the large dresses of this period. Compact sofas which look like two upholstered chairs fixed together, known as love chairs, were popular in the early and mid-19th century, as in the buttoned example here. Chesterfields, which were fully upholstered pieces with the arms and back the same height, became popular from the 1880s.*

FIG 2.26: During the second half of the 19th century, *reproductions of Georgian chairs by Chippendale, Hepplewhite and Sheraton were very popular (left). The Gothic revival, which was fashionable from the 1850s to 70s, resulted in furniture with pointed arches, tracery patterns, coats of arms and quatrefoils (four round lobed openings) as in this compact hall chair (right).*

FIG 2.27: From the 1870s *designers found inspiration from new sources to create daringly new pieces of furniture. The aesthetic style was heavily influenced by Japanese art and design and chairs with ebonised frames and oriental decorative backs were at the cutting edge of fashion. Arts and Crafts furniture makers rejected the machine and reinterpreted old rustic styles to create honest pieces of simple form using traditional materials, as in this chair (left) made from oak with a rush-work seat. Art Nouveau embraced modern materials but cast them into sinuous forms with natural foliage and graceful figurines. Charles Rennie Mackintosh influenced this style but preferred more geometric forms with thin vertical lines, gentle curves and decoration limited to simple motifs, with many of his chairs having distinctive tall backs (right).*

TABLES

Dining tables, occasional tables and games tables

The table is one of the oldest forms of furniture, providing a raised surface on which to prepare food, eat a meal and write or work upon. The type and style of legs, the timber used in its construction, and the shape and decoration of the top can all help in narrowing down the date when a table was made.

In its simplest form, the table is comprised of a series of planks resting upon trestles (a rigid frame historically of a triangular shape), a type which became standard in medieval and Tudor halls, as it could be easily dismantled and put up against a wall to clear the room for other activities. In the 16th century, as the rich divided their houses and created private chambers, a large, permanent type with fixed legs held together by stretchers, referred to as refectory tables (after those used by monks in their refectories), became fashionable. In the 17th century gateleg tables were introduced, with flaps held up by hinged legs which allowed the piece to be moved up against the wall when a meal was finished. This flexible form was used as a single piece until later in the century when it became fashionable to dine on two tables pushed together.

In the 18th century a wider range of tables became available, tailored to suit the increasing number of leisure activities in the homes of the wealthy. Cards and games tables, tea and coffee tables and a variety of small and occasional tables which could be rearranged or moved out of the way became popular. Lavishly decorated side and pier tables, the latter which were sited between the two large sash windows at the front of many 18th century homes, both came into fashion (those which could be fixed to the wall were referred to as console tables).

By the early 19th century, the homes of the wealthy began to be divided up into a larger number of rooms with a specific role, hence tables and chairs became fixed items which were left in

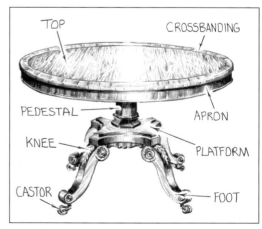

FIG 3.1: A Regency *pedestal dining table with labels of its key parts.*

place when finished with. Taking a meal at a single, large dining table came back into fashion. These tables could have hefty pedestals supporting them now they did not have to be moved out of the way.

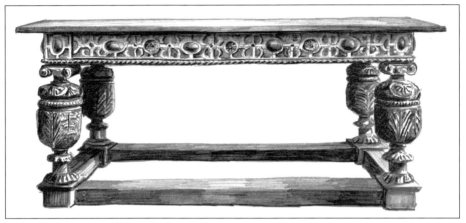

FIG 3.2: Elizabethan and Jacobean refectory tables *typically had a large rectangular top comprising two or three wide planks with a simple square edge. The legs had distinctive acorn-like centre sections (referred to as cup and cover) which were decorated with carvings of foliage, scrolls and geometric patterns. The stretchers which supported the bottom of the legs were close to the ground and the apron often featured a string of motifs or carvings of arches (lunettes) or strapwork as in the example above. In the early 17th century the bulbous legs become less pronounced and the decoration becomes more refined although the overall form remains similar.*

FIG 3.3: Gateleg tables *with hinged flaps held up by swinging legs or pull out bars were developed during the mid-17th century. Early types had a large round top of about 8ft (2400mm) with a square edge and simple turned legs. After the Restoration of 1660, legs carved with a spiral, sometimes with bobbin-turned stretchers, became the height of fashion and tables were generally reduced in diameter.*

FIG 3.4: Side tables *in the late 17th century gave craftsmen the opportunity to display their skills. The tops could be made of marble, figured walnut or marquetry, as in this example. Some had a drawer set within a formal apron while the finest could have elaborate carving. Straight, scrolled and spiral legs were popular often with flat stretchers in an 'x' shape. Sometimes the junction of these had a circular section upon which a vase could be mounted.*

FIG 3.5: By the early 18th century *gateleg tables had elegant cabriole legs which gave diners more leg room, as in this example. Walnut was the timber of choice in the Queen Anne period but as it was not easy to carve its attractive burr and graining was put on show. The top now could have a rounded or profiled edge and a border around the perimeter made by placing strips of veneer at right angles to the outer edge called crossbanding. This became a feature of many of the finest wood tables throughout the 18th century.*

FIG 3.6: Games tables *began to be made from the late 17th century. Formerly gateleg tables had been used but the stretchers got in the way of players hence new games tables were developed with cabriole legs and clever pull-out mechanisms to support flaps. The top could be reversible with backgammon one side, as in this example, and a sheet of fabric or, by the early 18th century, baise on the other. The corners of the top usually had round or square blocks on which candles could be mounted, a drawer might be provided below for games and wells were sometimes fitted for keeping money safe.*

FIG 3.7: By the early Georgian period *side tables had evolved with cabriole or scrolled legs and an apron which featured a central pendant or feature. This example, based upon the designs of William Kent, which were popular in the 1730s and 40s, has a top made of polished marble with a richly decorated gilt frame (some were white with gilt details) with shells, acanthus leaves, trails of bellflowers and a female mask in the centre. Some of the finest tables had realistically carved animals supporting the top which could also be made of faux*

marble, veneer or had a Japanned finish as marquetry fell from favour. Gesso (see glossary) was a cheaper alternative to carving wood, with size and gypsum paste applied to the surface and the patterns punched, incised or raised up before the gilt was applied.

FIG 3.8: Taking tea at home *with friends and guests became fashionable from the 1730s and in response manufacturers produced small round tables, some with a raised edge known as pie crust tables. These evolved into a range of small tables including supper tables and dumb waiters (see Chapter 8) with various tiers for holding a silver kettle, plates and food. This example with its pedestal and tripod legs was possibly first created by Thomas Chippendale.*

FIG 3.9: Pembrokes *were a very popular form of occasional table in the 18th century with a square or oval top, a central section with drawers and a drop leaf either side which could be held up by brackets. These versatile pieces were used for needlework, writing and drawing, as well as taking a light meal. This example from the 1790s in the style of Hepplewhite had tapered straight legs and mahogany with inlay and brass castors.*

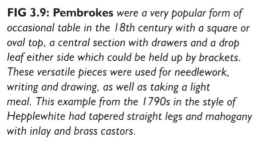

FIG 3.10: By the second half of the 18th century *dining at a single table was once again the norm. A popular, versatile form had a central section with flaps either side which could be raised up with two half-moon tables added at either end as shown in this example. The two ends could also make a smaller round table or the central part could be used on its own.*

FIG 3.11: Side tables *with an elegant and restrained curvaceous form are distinctive of the 1760s and 70s. They often featured decorative patterns in the veneer as marquetry came back into fashion. Mahogany fell from favour as satinwood and rosewood proved popular timbers.*

FIG 3.12: Robert Adam designed side tables *with a semi-circular marble or patterned inlayed wood top and a gilt, white or pastel-coloured frame usually with a central feature like an oval medallion framed by swags. This example features urns, paterae and swags of husks with fluted tapering legs making for a light and elegant piece distinctive of the late 18th century. Hepplewhite created similar designs but preferred simple fluted friezes, less busy patterns on the top and did not feature carved figures.*

FIG 3.13: Sheraton's small tables *often featured colourful medallions on the inlayed top and delicate floral painting on the legs. He also designed sofa tables, a popular piece in the Regency period, which was longer than a Pembroke table usually with two drawers rather than one, which were used for writing, drawing and reading while reclining in a sofa. This example has legs at each end with brass lion's paw castors but by the 1810's a central pedestal leg was popular.*

FIG 3.14: Regency dining tables *tend to be heavier pieces compared with late 18th-century types with oval, round or rectangular tops supported upon single or twin pedestals. The latter had large pillars often with downswept legs featuring prominent knees and brass end caps and castors in the form of animal claws or paws, as in this example. Mahogany, rosewood and walnut sometimes with brass, pearl or exotic wood inlays were fashionable.*

FIG 3.15: Victorian tables *were heavier in appearance than preceding styles with richer carving on the legs and more complex designs on the top. Many dining tables in this period had rectangular tops with curved corners and features that copied earlier styles as on this example with bulbous Jacobean legs.*

FIG 3.16: Arts and Crafts designers *created refreshingly simple tables with plain tops and strong oak frames with decoration limited to enlivening structural parts. Hearts, spades, vertical lines and geometric shapes were popular details. Even the more elaborate pieces still retained this approach.*

Legs, feet and castors

The type of legs and feet on furniture can be a useful key to their style and date. Elizabethan tables have distinctive squat and bulbous legs often with large cup and cover elements, later Jacobean turned legs become more restrained and thinner. After the Restoration, scrolled and twisted legs were used on chairs and some tables, and inverted cup or trumpet legs could also be found on the latter. In the Queen Anne period the cabriole leg became fashionable on tables, chairs and other pieces, usually with a simple, pad-like foot, but in the finest early Georgian examples more elaborate ball and claw feet were used. Straight tapered legs became popular in the late 18th century, usually with a fluted (concave lines) shaft and a reeded (convex lines) one on some Regency types. Sabre legs are another distinctive style from this latter period. Victorian legs came in a wide variety of forms to suit the style of the piece, cabriole legs with moulding all the way down the leg were common on balloon back chairs, clustered columns were seen on Gothic revival pieces and heavy turned or gadrooned baluster legs on many tables.

Heavier furniture like cabinets and bookcases had shorter more robust feet. 17th-century pieces usually had bun or ball shaped feet. Straight-edged bracket feet became popular in the early Georgian period, more graceful ogee ('s' shaped) outer edges were fashionable in the middle of the 18th century. More simple splay-shaped bracket feet suited Neoclassical pieces while turned feet were common on Victorian furniture.

Castors with wheels to make it easier to move furniture around a room were introduced from the 1740s. At first they had leather discs forming the wheel within the brass fitting, but these were soon superseded by proper wheels. The shape of the socket into which the leg or foot fitted was determined by the latter's form, although decorated box or claw types were a distinctive feature of the Regency period.

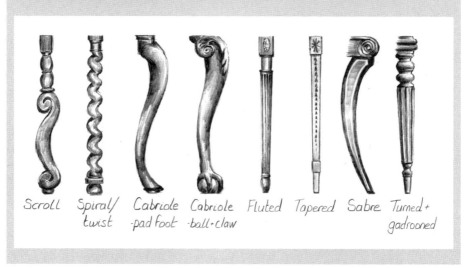

Scroll   Spiral/   Cabriole   Cabriole   Fluted   Tapered   Sabre   Turned +
          twist   ·pad foot   ·ball·claw   gadrooned

DESKS

Bureaux, writing tables and secretaires

Writing and reading was an occupation mainly limited to the clergy in medieval times, only becoming more generally practised by gentlemen and ladies from the 16th century. Table top writing boxes which, when opened, revealed a sloping surface to work upon can be found from the Tudor period. It was not until the late 17th century that larger pieces of furniture specifically designed for reading and writing began to appear as developing trade, industry, banking, and the civil service created an increase in the amount of paper records, letters and documents. Bureaux, desks and writing tables were designed in response to this demand. At that time too, wealthy gentlemen began to collect books and manuscripts, at first displayed in a simple cabinet but by the 18th century in a library, a masculine room in which they could work in private or meet guests while showing off the finest parts of their collection. High-quality tables on which books could be displayed and large desks for writing were made for this room, often with false doors and drawers on the back so it could be located in the centre of the room.

The general form of bureaux changed little over the following centuries other than the details that reflected the latest styles. Desks and writing tables had greater variety as new types were introduced. Some were more feminine

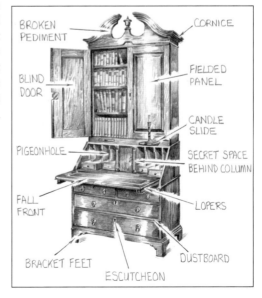

FIG 4.1: A bureau bookcase *from the 1740s with labels of its key parts. The doors could be solid (blind) so the contents were hidden from view, as in this case with a rectangular frame and a central panel with sloping edges (fielded). Alternatively the doors could be glazed with patterns formed out of the glazing bars. These compact bureau bookcases appear from the late 17th century and were popular in reproduction form during the Victorian period.*

BROKEN PEDIMENT
CORNICE
BLIND DOOR
FIELDED PANEL
CANDLE SLIDE
PIGEONHOLE
SECRET SPACE BEHIND COLUMN
FALL FRONT
LOPERS
BRACKET FEET
DUSTBOARD
ESCUTCHEON

in form as writing letters and notes became fashionable, or were more compact to suit the more numerous but smaller rooms in many houses from the late 18th century. Some pieces were designed to be portable so small bureaux and desks can be found with handles on the sides so they could be moved when the owner went travelling or off to sea. In the 19th century, as the middle classes sought to emulate their social superiors, so compact bureaux with glass-fronted bookcases above became a popular addition in urban homes where a library would be out of the question.

FIG 4.2: Writing boxes or slopes *can be found from the Tudor period onwards and provided a portable surface to work upon plus storage for pens, ink and paper. By the 17th century they were often mounted on a stand and later in the century evolved into the bureau, with or without a cabinet or bookcase above. This campaign writing slope, with its distinctive flush brass handles, is from the early 19th century. It has an angled opening to make one large sloping surface when fully open, with ink wells and pen storage at the top and a paper drawer underneath. Some had metal candle stands which could be fitted into the side or top.*

FIG 4.3: An early form *of cabinet with a writing table was the secretaire, escritoire, or secretary. This provided a pull-down door from the upper section which provided the flat writing surface and exposed a series of drawers, pigeon holes and cupboards inside with drawers below. These were introduced in the late 17th and early 18th century, as in this example, with a variety of systems to support the desk and arrangements of doors and drawers. Some later examples had a recess (kneehole) in the middle to provide leg room.*

FIG 4.4: Bureaux *(from the French word for 'office') developed in the late 17th century and were, in effect, writing boxes set upon a chest of drawers. They proved more popular in England than the secretaire and their general form remained largely unchanged during the 18th and 19th century, with the fall front hinged on the bottom and resting upon loppers when open to reveal small drawers and pigeon holes within. On the earliest types, the upper sloping section was made separately with a moulding covering up the joint between this and the chest of drawers below, as in this William and Mary example. This moulding was a feature up until the 1730s even though by this time bureaux*

were made in one piece. Bun feet were originally fitted but by the early 18th century bracket feet were common although some later, lighter pieces were raised off the ground on cabriole legs.

FIG 4.5: The kneehole desk *was introduced at the beginning of the 18th century. They were compact writing tables with two sets of drawers either side and a central kneehole usually with a recessed cupboard at the back, as in this walnut Queen Anne example. From the mid-18th century, pedestal desks, which were larger and had more substantial sets of drawers either side, became popular. Those in a library, where the back would be exposed, had false drawer or cupboard fronts on the rear.*

FIG 4.7: Writing desks *had developed from the mid-17th century, a distinctive early form popular in France was the bureau plat, a large table with drawers set within the frieze below the top. As letter and note writing became all the craze with the Georgian upper classes so compact elegant kneehole desks and writing tables with one or two rows of drawers set upon carved legs became fashionable. This example from the 1750s with richly shaped cabriole legs was referred to as a library desk and has drawers and door fronts on all four faces as all sides were visible when positioned in the centre of the room.*

FIG 4.6: Bureau cabinets *were a popular combination in the 18th and 19th centuries. This example from the 1790s is in satinwood and mahogany with a roll top or tambour shutter, thin tapered legs, gothic ogee arched glazing bars and a broken pediment – all fashionable details of this period.*

FIG 4.8: In the Regency period *small portable desks were fashionable. Some had cylinder tops with a rigid curved lid and a pull out writing surface. Another distinctive form was the kidney-shaped desk, as in this Sheraton-style example, which could also could be used as a dressing table.*

FIG 4.10: Small portable desks *were sometimes designed for naval officers so they could be taken with them when they went to sea. The compact type pictured here was originally made for Captain Davenport in the 1790s and had a sliding top section which could pull forward for writing with a series of drawers, compartments and slide out flaps fitted in the sides. This clever piece was popular throughout the 19th century especially in ladies rooms, although later Victorian types often had the top fixed with an overhang at the front supported on a pair of richly carved scroll legs.*

FIG 4.9: Carlton House desks *were another distinctive form from the Regency period. Based upon a design from one at the Prince Regent's London residence of Carlton House, they had a U-shaped bank of drawers set upon a rectangular or curved desk top. In the example here, the centre can be angled upwards to form an easel.*

FIG 4.11: Drum tables *with drawers set into the frieze and a central pedestal with three or four legs was a popular feature for the centre of the library in the early 19th century.*

FIG 4.12: Pedestal desks *which became popular from the mid-18th century have changed little in their general form ever since. Some were finished on all four sides for use as a library desk, others were extra deep so two people could work facing each other, known as partner desks. Victorian versions, as in this example, had a leather-covered top with rounded corners and turned wooden knobs on the drawers rather than brass handles, which was fashionable on many pieces of furniture in this period.*

Robert Adam

The son of the Scottish architect William Adam, Robert Adam gained much of his experience in building while working with his family. In 1754 he set forth on his Grand Tour, a journey taking four years around the architectural wonders of Ancient Rome, before establishing his own business back in London with his brother James. The Adam brothers developed a new style which broke with the formal and rigid proportions of the Palladian style and created buildings and interiors full of movement with domes, arched niches and bowed fronts. A key part of Adam's skill was his control of the whole project from the plan of the house down to the design of the furniture to adorn his elegant interiors. Delicate and shallow Classical mouldings with medallions, urns, vine scrolls, garlands of husks, swags and ribbons and the careful use of pastel colours make his interiors unique. Although he did not make pieces himself he employed some of the leading cabinet makers of the day to complete his designs including Thomas Chippendale. His early style of interiors and furniture reflects much of the Rococo which was still fashionable when he started out in business, but by 1780 his style becomes less ornate and purer in form heralding in the Neoclassical style which would dominate the Regency period.

CHESTS

Chests of drawers, coffers and tallboys

The chest, in its basic form, was a rectangular box with a lid with the earliest examples carved out a tree trunk. By the 13th century, these chests or coffers were usually formed from planks held in place by iron straps or nails until improved construction methods using mortise and tenon joints became common in the 15th century. They were used by the nobility to transport valuable belongings like clothes and plate between their various properties and by the church for storing vestments, with the finest Tudor examples made from exotic woods with richly carved panels.

As it was difficult to get to items stored at the bottom of a chest, new types with drawers set in the lower section became popular in the early 17th century and by the time of the Restoration, these had evolved into the chest of drawers. At this time, the idea of case construction was imported from the continent whereby a cheap wood like oak or pine was used to form the carcass and then veneered in walnut. It was not long before these important storage pieces were developed, with examples set upon a stand by the end of the century. Alternatively, they could be formed as a double-stacked chest on chest, also referred to as a tallboy, which was a popular form during the Georgian period. By the mid-18th century mahogany was the fashionable timber, with at first a serpentine, rococo shape and then later in the century a gentle bowing front being popular. In the finest houses, a richly decorated chest of drawers, sometimes with hinged doors across the front known as a commode, was designed specifically for the drawing room or salon (see FIG 5.6).

By the Regency period a wide range

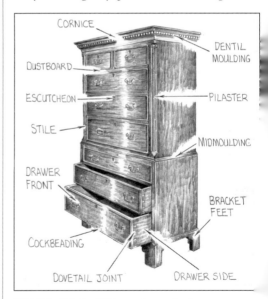

FIG 5.1: A late 18th-century *chest on chest, also referred to as a tallboy, with labels of its parts.*

34

of pieces had been developed in various shapes and sizes. Military chests had brass-bounded corners and flush-fitting handles, semaines (from the French word for a week) had seven drawers designed to hold a week's worth of clothing, and Wellington chests were similar, but had a vertical column up both sides, one of which was hinged and held the drawers shut when it was locked. Victorian pieces could be found in a wide range of forms and woods, with revival styles and ancient coffers adding to the mix.

FIG 5.2: The earliest examples of chests or coffers *were typically made from large oak planks held together by iron straps and nails. They often stood upon the side panels, which were extended down below the base (top). During the 15th century a new style, which had panels joined by mortise and tenon joints, was introduced (centre). The finest examples could be made from exotic woods with richly carved panels featuring the latest Renaissance or older Gothic motifs. In the early 17th century a distinctive type, with carved designs of buildings turreted on the front panel, was made by German craftsmen who had settled in South London. As the carvings looked like Henry VIII's Nonsuch Palace they were later termed Nonsuch chests. Plain panelled coffers soon became the norm, some with drawers below to access the awkward-to-reach base (bottom).*

FIG 5.3: Early chests *were made from a framework with mortise and tenon joints and panels inserted between. After the Restoration, Charles II brought over craftsmen from Europe who introduced case construction, whereby a timber carcass was made from a cheaper wood like pine or oak that was glued and nailed together and then usually veneered in a fine quality timber like walnut, some with marquetry patterns. Along with this were new styles and forms including the chest on stand: a chest of drawers, sometimes with a cupboard, raised up on legs. The William and Mary-style piece in this example has the distinctive barley twist legs, horizontal wavy stretchers and drop handles which are distinctive of the late 17th century. The earliest drawer boxes were usually supported on runners which fitted in grooves along their sides, but by the 1690s they had*

thin bearers along the bottom which supported them underneath. The drawer fronts at this date began to be dovetailed to the box and if there was any moulding around the edges then it was fixed to the carcass.

FIG 5.4: In the first half of the 18th century *chests on stands fell from favour and were replaced by chests on chests or tallboys. They usually had a flat cornice, and a mid moulding covering up the gap between the separate upper and lower sections. Earlier Queen Anne examples had walnut veneer, which on the finest examples was carefully selected to make the figuring in the wood symmetrical, with bun or ball feet and pear drop or bail handles. By the time of George II, mahogany, bracket feet and swan neck handles were in fashion, as in this example, and moulding was now fixed around the edges of the drawer front rather than the carcass, usually with a quarter circle shape called ovolo.*

FIG 5.5: In the mid-18th century *French Rococo pieces with a bulbous form of wavy sides and fronts, referred to as bombé chests, were fashionable. However, these were too extreme for many, so more restrained types with just a serpentine front became popular in England. This example has elaborate swan handles and escutcheons and a fretwork pattern in the style of Chippendale down the canted (angled) stiles. There is also a thin 'brushing slide' just below the top which could be pulled out so clothes could be brushed clean upon it. From the 1750s it was usual for the grain of the drawer bottom to run from side to side rather than front to back as it formerly had. Cockbeading, a thin lip to the drawer front, was a popular moulding from the 1760s (see FIG 5.1).*

FIG 5.6: For the most luxurious homes *in the mid-18th century a commode, a richly decorated chest of drawers, was a must. They had evolved in the early 1700s in France and became fashionable in England by the 1740s with a serpentine or bombé form and a veneered top (marble was more common on the continent). Those in the 1740s and 50s had mahogany veneer or a decorative Japanned finish, while in the 1760s and 70s painted or marquetry designs*

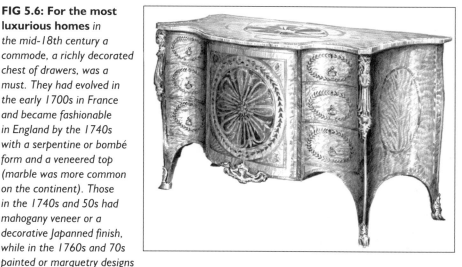

on the fronts and tops were in vogue. Ormolu mounts (gilded metal decorative pieces) were a fashionable addition which capped the edges, friezes and legs of commodes in this period, as in the example here. These high-status pieces which allowed the cabinet makers to display their full talents are amongst the most valuable pieces of furniture today.

FIG 5.8: Bow-fronted, *half-moon shape commodes with delicate Classical motifs in the style of Adam and Sheraton were fashionable in the late 18th century. This example has a veneered front featuring a painted roundel with an ormolu frieze and tapered legs, which are typical of the age. Rectangular forms came back into fashion during the Regency period, some with lion's paw feet. By this period the term commode drops from common usage for these elaborate, sideboard-like chests of drawers and by the mid-Victorian period the term was widely used to describe close stools, small cupboards or stands in which a chamber pot could be discreetly stored.*

FIG 5.7: From the 1770s *shallow bow fronts to chests of drawers and commodes became fashionable. Tallboys, as in this early 19th century example, fell from favour in many homes and were often split into their two sections and used as separate chests of drawers.*

Thomas Hope

Born in Amsterdam to a wealthy banking family, Thomas Hope did not enter the family business but instead immersed himself in the arts and wide-ranging Grand Tours which included parts of Asia and Africa. He and his brothers were forced to flee Amsterdam in 1795 when French Revolutionary forces invaded Holland, and they settled in a property in London designed by Robert Adam. Hope used it to display his collection and ideas for interior design, a phrase first coined by him. In 1807 he published *Household Furniture and Interior Decoration* which introduced a new Classical style that was to help shape furniture design during the Regency period.

FIG 5.9: Semainers were tall, *thin chests for storing clothes with seven drawers, one for each day of the week (from the French word semaine meaning 'week'). A variation of this piece which was popular throughout the 19th century was the Wellington chest which has the addition of a hinged and lockable column up the side (shown open on the right of this example) which would secure all the drawers at once. They can be found with a variety of number of drawers and were often used to keep valuable collections.*

FIG 5.10: Campaign chests *were specifically designed for an army officer's belongings while on service abroad during the 19th century. They could be split into an upper and lower section with flush-fitting handles, brass bindings on corners and joints and detachable legs to protect it whilst on the move, as in this example. Victorian chests of drawers became a feature primarily of the bedroom and were included in the suites of furniture that could be purchased in a myriad of styles during the period. By the turn of the 20th century, machine-cut dovetail joints and carving are common (they are not irregular as is earlier handmade work) and the dustboards between the drawers fall from favour as runners up the side of the drawer box come back into fashion.*

Handles

It was not until drawers and cupboard doors became a common feature on furniture from the mid-17th century that much thought went into the decorative potential of handles. Early pieces usually had wooden knobs and if any metal was used it was typically made from hammered ironwork. In the William and Mary period brass handles, usually in the form of a teardrop hung from a small round or shaped backplate, came into fashion (top left). Bail handles, with a ring hung off a backplate, became popular in the Queen Anne period and the latter could be round or have a decorative shaped form with a longer D-shaped ring (top centre), often featuring a pierced pattern. By the mid-18th century, bail handles with pronounced swan neck-shaped ends fitted into two separate backplates or roses were becoming popular (top right), some of which could be cast or pierced with Rococo or fretwork designs. By the 1780s new techniques for making brass meant that handles looked more like gold and lost the pitting that characterises earlier types. Round or oval bail handles, with a ring which fitted into a recess around the edge of a matching-sized backplate, came into fashion around this time (bottom left). In the Regency period, bail handles with squared-off ends or rings held in the mouth of lion-shaped backplates (bottom centre) were popular. By the early Victorian period, turned wooden knobs had once again become fashionable, some later types having coloured inserts, while porcelain knobs were introduced in the 1850s, some with painted decoration. Arts and Crafts designers revived hammered ironwork and produced beautifully crafted metal handles, escutcheons and strap hinges to embellish their work, while handles with serpentine shapes made from copper (bottom right) were an Art Nouveau detail found in the early 20th century.

CABINETS

Cupboards, bookcases and sideboards

In medieval homes, the earliest types of cupboard were built into the wall and were used for valuables and precious food stuffs. Those in churches used to store the chalice and other valuables were called an aumbry, although this title was applied widely in the past to most built-in cupboards. In the Tudor and Jacobean period, court cupboards and buffets were introduced: sturdy oak tables with small cupboards and shelves to hold dinnerware and on which to serve food. Low cupboards or hutches were raised up on legs and could be used for a variety of tasks. Some were used to keep the household staff's rations and are referred to as dole cupboards. Presses were a larger piece with doors and featured shelves for linen and pegs to hang clothes, the forerunner of the wardrobe (see Chapter 7).

By the early 18th century the range of furniture for storage, display and the serving of food had expanded to reflect the wider range of interests and busier social life of the gentry. Young men began exploring Europe on Grand Tours and bringing back with them relics of the Classical past and mementos of their journey. Cabinets in which they could be displayed were an important feature in the house. As the upper classes began to turn their minds to matters of science and the arts so they collected books covering these subjects in addition to those which formed part of their Classical education. Bookcases, from compact pieces for a few books in the corner of a reception room to banks of large shelved pieces for a library, became a standard feature of large 18th-century houses.

Dining was now a more refined experience, so the rustic and chunky court cupboards, buffets and dressers

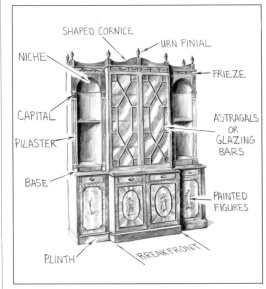

FIG 6.1: A late 18th century bookcase *with a breakfront, a central section standing forward, labelled with some of the key parts.*

of the Tudor and Jacobean period were now replaced by more elegant serving tables and later by sideboards, which by the Victorian period had expanded to become vast pieces with tall backs featuring mirrors and shelves. However, at the end of the 19th century the Arts and Crafts movement not only introduced refreshingly simple and honest furniture for storage but also made items like dressers and chests, which had formerly been relegated to service rooms, into acceptable pieces to be sited in a reception room.

FIG 6.2: A popular Tudor and Jacobean *piece used for storage and display was the court cupboard. It was originally a board for cup, crockery and pewter plate (hence cupboard) and as they were generally not very high they were termed court, from the French word for short. They featured in the homes of the well-off from the Elizabethan period through to the mid-17th century, although they were still made later than this. Most had a three-tier form, with 16th century examples featuring distinctive bulbous legs (although these become thinner and more restrained in the next century), and a canted (angled) storage space in the upper section is a common feature. Similar pieces which are fully enclosed and had shelves and pegs inside for clothes are known as presses.*

FIG 6.3: A buffet *was similar to a court cupboard, comprising two or three tiers, on which meals were served in a private chamber or dining room. They would often have drawers built into the decorative frieze across the front. This example dates from the 1630s and has turned legs with less pronounced features than Elizabethan versions (as in FIG 6.2).*

FIG 6.4: Some cupboards completely enclosed by doors were used for storing food, and would have an air vent in the front usually covered by little spindles. In the 16th century the doors could be decorated with deep carving featuring central roundels with the raised silhouette of a head (Romayne work). In the early 17th century, geometric patterns were fashionable, as in this Jacobean example. Later in the century, plain panels were common.

FIG 6.5: Following the restoration of 1660, a serving table began to replace the buffet in fashionable dining rooms. It was long and thin in form with a row of drawers below. A more rustic version, usually termed a dresser, as in this late 17th century example, was popular in large rural homes and would later evolve into the more familiar piece with shelves above.

FIG 6.6: Chinese lacquer cabinets were the most desirable piece of furniture in the late 17th and early 18th century. They were small cupboards imported from the Far East with a black, red or green background and oriental lacquered paintings of trees, animals, and buildings across the front. These cabinets were prized by wealthy gentlemen and used to display their private collections of coins and curiosities. At first they would have sat upon a table, but from around 1690 they had special stands made in England for them, some with fashionable barley twist, turned baluster or double-scrolled legs, as in this example. Alternatively, they could be mounted upon richly carved gilt stands. Similar cabinets were also made in fine quality wood with marquetry designs across the doors.

FIG 6.7: By the late 17th century *new elegant cabinets with a chest of drawers or a bureau beneath a pair of solid doors became fashionable. William and Mary examples tend to have a flat cornice along the top. Later Queen Anne ones had a hooped or shaped top, as in this example, with a pair of mirrored doors. Doors with clear glass held in place by glazing bars were introduced from the early 18th century. The finest examples were embellished with marquetry designs. The earliest ones tend to have a stronger contrast than those from the Queen Anne period. An intricate foliage pattern known as seaweed, introduced in the 1690s, is distinctive of this decade. Corner cupboards which had originally been built into the panelling of some earlier rooms were replaced by freestanding corner cabinets in this period.*

FIG 6.8: At first, bookcases were combined with bureaux *and chests of drawers but by the 1740s dedicated large mahogany pieces with breakfronts were designed specifically for libraries. In this early Georgian period, they were often treated as an architectural piece in the style of William Kent, with broken pediments and urns along the top, and bracketed scrolls and fluted pilasters flanking the doors or open shelving. The line of small squares under the cornice is known as a 'dentil' feature, which came into fashion in this period but is not exclusive to it. Doors could be fitted with small rectangular panes of glass but by the middle of the century glazing bars were formed into decorative patterns inspired by the designs of Thomas Chippendale, as in this example. Earlier smaller pieces could stand upon bun, ball or simple bracketed feet but later breakfront pieces usually had a plinth, as in this example.*

FIG 6.9: In the 1740s *cabinets and bookcases with mirror glass doors were more common, but in the following decades clear glass, held in place by glazing bars which were often arranged in decorative patterns, became the norm. Broken pediments were fitted along the top, some with distinctive fretwork patterns, as in this example, which was a feature used by Chippendale. Most cabinets were mounted on straight bracket feet although the finest had an undulating ogee shape. Cabinets specifically designed for displaying china appeared in this period, possibly the creation of Chippendale, and encoignures which were small French-style corner cupboards became fashionable in the second half of the century.*

FIG 6.10: By the late 18th century *serving tables had evolved into the more familiar sideboard. Robert Adam set a pair of pedestals at each end of a table with urns mounted on top, which could hold iced or hot water, as part of his dining room suites. Single piece, pedestal-style sideboards with cupboards in either end were popular during the Regency period. By the 1780s more compact sideboards with drawers below the polished top became a standard feature in the finest homes. They*

could have a flat, bowed or serpentine front, as in this Regency example, usually with a central cutlery drawer and drawers or cupboards either side. These often had a baise lining to protect plate or a lead lining to keep drinks cool. In the Regency period, it was common to have a brass rail along the back from which would hang a short curtain to prevent splashes from serving food and drinks marking the wall covering behind.

FIG 6.11: Small side cabinets *became fashionable from the late 18th century. Those with a display shelf above and drawer below, as in this example, are known as chiffoniers. Larger, more elaborate designs, often with curved glazed doors at either end, are referred to as credenzas. A vitrine (from the French word for glass) is an elegant glass display cabinet which is usually glazed on three sides and often raised up on legs. All these types of cabinets remained popular during the 19th century.*

FIG 6.12: Regency bookcases and cabinets *often had brass or gilt trellis across the fronts, brass galleries at the rear and patterns formed from thin brass inlays set into the wood. Pleated silk was neatly arranged behind the wire grill to protect the contents from light and dust. This example from the early 1800s has brass paw-shaped feet and tapering columns, which is distinctive of the fashionable Egyptian style.*

FIG 6.13: By the late Regency period *cabinets and sideboards become heavier in appearance and the latter now featured low backboards rather than curtains on rails. In the Victorian period, backboards grew in height to feature mirrors, shelving and lavish carved decoration as in this Jacobean-styled example. Gothic revival pieces often featured pointed arches and medieval motifs in the door and back panels.*

Thomas Shearer
This notable cabinet maker and skilled draughtsman was based in London and he probably influenced the work of both Hepplewhite and Sheraton, although his name is less well known. Shearer's *The Cabinet Maker's London Book of Prices and Designs of Cabinet Work* of 1788 included drawings for sideboards as a single piece, the first examples of it in this familiar form. His pieces usually had fine curves and elegant legs, and he had a preference for simplicity in design. Further editions of his book were made over the following decades as it remained influential into the Regency period.

FIG 6.14: The dresser *evolved from the tables with a line of drawers popular in the 17th century to the more familiar base unit with shelving and cupboards above. At the same time it was relegated from the dining room to the kitchen in the finest houses and most antique examples would have been designed for the service rooms of a large house or were country pieces for farmhouses and rural properties. The rustic oak dresser was made fashionable by Arts and Crafts designers in the late 19th century, as in this example.*

FIG 6.15: Arts and Crafts furniture designers *were creating pieces which were more than just a revival of old styles and methods of construction. They used vernacular forms of furniture to inspire new designs composed of clean lines, simple forms and plain surfaces which allowed the beauty of the natural wood to be displayed. Decoration was limited to the functional parts like the hinges and handles. Simple foliage designs and heart-shaped motifs often featured and long strap hinges were a favourite form sometimes in hand-wrought iron rather than brass. This example by C. F. A. Voysey has a medieval-style pastoral scene formed in the enlarged central strap hinge.*

FIG 6.16: Art Deco *is a broad title for the new styles which developed in the inter-war years. In the 1920s, pieces often had a stepped form and the finest furniture had exotic and richly decorated surfaces (left) inspired by the latest French designs and a craze for Egyptian motifs after the discovery of Tutankhamun's tomb. In the 1930s, streamline forms became fashionable and resulted in distinctive curved pieces of furniture (right).*

Marquetry and inlays

At various times since the Tudor period it has been fashionable for some of the finest pieces of furniture to feature decorative patterns set into the surface of the wood. Inlaying is an ancient technique which was fashionable on some of the finest pieces of Tudor and Restoration furniture. It was formed by cutting spaces into the surface of the solid wood and inlaying pieces of contrasting timber, ivory, mother of pearl or bone to create a small pattern. As case furniture with a veneered surface came into fashion in the late 17th century so a new technique referred to as marquetry began to replace it (simple geometric patterns formed out of wood are sometimes referred to as parquetry). Thin sheets of wood were cut into shapes and glued to the carcass to form the pattern, with the intricate fine foliage design known as seaweed being distinctive of the 1690s. Boulle work, named after the French cabinetmaker André Charles Boulle who worked for Louis XIV, is the most elaborate form of marquetry and inlay with fabulous designs formed using tortoiseshell, brass and pewter. Marquetry and inlays fell from fashion in the early 18th century as plain walnut and mahogany veneers which displayed their rich figuring was popular until the 1770s, when it once again became a feature of the new Neoclassical pieces. Brass inlay, in which a thin strip of brass is set within the wood to make simple patterns, became fashionable from the 1790s and is distinctive of Regency furniture.

BEDS

Four-posters, presses and wardrobes

The bedroom has not always been the warm and private retreat filled with a wide range of furniture we are familiar with today. Originally the lord of the manor would sleep on the floor of his hall along with his household. It was only in the later medieval period that private chambers became common so he could escape the noise and smell. Even in the Tudor period these would have seemed bare by modern standards with the room dominated by a four-poster bed, its bed hangings or curtains helping to keep out the cold draughts and give the occupants some privacy.

In some late 17th century country houses, the bedchamber was positioned at the end of a long straight range of rooms called an enfilade and was designed so the owner could receive friends and guests here, a fashion which continued into the following century. By this date, the beds in the finest houses had developed from the richly carved oak pieces of the Tudor period into magnificent displays of upholstered bed hangings on the finest state beds. An alternative fashion was to set the bed within an alcove which could be curtained off so it did not require a canopy on posts. In the late 18th century, beds with a short canopy fitted with draped fabrics, known as a half tester, became fashionable but it was not until the 19th century when the bedroom had become a private reserve of the family that conventional wooden, iron and brass bed frames with just a head and footboard became standard.

Until the mid-18th century bedroom furniture was usually limited to chests and linen presses. It was only around this date that washing daily became fashionable and washstands made an appearance. Dressing tables were

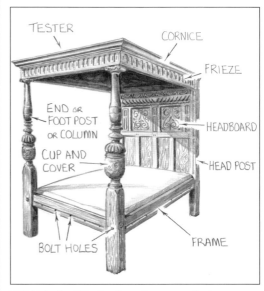

FIG 7.1: An Elizabethan *four-poster bed with labels of its parts.*

49

literally a table covered by a cloth in many households; purpose-made pieces with drawers and a mirror only became common in the later Georgian period. The modern wardrobe evolved in the early 19th century from the linen press which continued to be available alongside it. It was therefore not until the Victorian period that wardrobes, chests of drawers, dressing tables and bedside cabinets became standard fittings in middle and upper class homes and these pieces were usually sold as a suite in a matching style

FIG 7.2: Four-poster beds *dominated the private bed chambers in wealthy Tudor and Jacobean homes. Their headboards and columns, which supported the tester or canopy from which curtains were hung, were richly carved on the finest pieces with coats of arms, bulbous cups and covers, and Romayne work. This Elizabethan example has round arched carvings on the ends and Renaissance features decorating the columns which are distinctive of the late 16th and early 17th century. In the Jacobean period, the emphasis began to switch onto hanging more lavish fabrics so there is less carving and the decoration is more subdued. The mattress could be supported on a mesh of ropes which were fed through bolt holes in the sides and ends (FIG 7.1), later straps and wooden slats became common.*

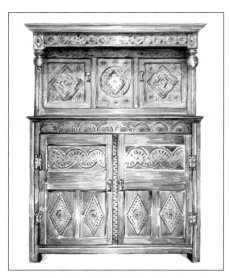

FIG 7.3: Although bed chambers *were relatively spartan there would usually be storage provided for clothes. This could include a simple chest (as in FIG 5.2) and a cupboard with doors. The latter, referred to as a press, was similar in form to the court cupboards (see FIG 6.2) but was fully enclosed and had shelves for linen and pegs for clothes. Early examples often had bulbous cup and cover balusters supporting the canopy across the top. In the second half of the 17th century, hanging pendants and less vigorous carving was often used, as in this example. These evolved into the clothes press in the 18th century, which was a more vertical piece usually with a chest of drawers in the base and a pair of doors on the upper half enclosing pull-out drawers.*

FIG 7.4: By the late 17th century *the fabrics which were hung from the bed for privacy and warmth had become the key decorative element and the quality of the piece was determined by the expense lavished on them. Some of the most magnificent were based upon engravings made by Daniel Marot, a designer for Louis XIV who fled persecution in France as a Protestant in 1685 and ended up working for William and Mary in London. In some of his influential designs he featured an angel tester which seemed to float above the bed as it was supported on chains from the ceiling rather than end posts. These grand state beds were an opportunity for the upholsterer to display his skills, as in this early 18th century example, and most parts of the structure were covered in luxurious fabric-like damasks and silks. By the 1730s, owners were growing tired of finding bed bugs in the fabrics, with the constant cleaning which these state beds required, so new mahogany four posters with panelled headboards and elegant fluted columns came into fashion.*

FIG 7.5: In the second half of the 18th century, *the linen or clothes press had become a popular piece in the bedroom. The upper section was a cupboard with slide-out drawers, as shown here, with fine veneered panels or carved mouldings. Oval shapes were fashionable, and on some Chippendale examples they had fretwork patterns carved down the angled corners of the frame (see FIG 5.5). Some of the finest had serpentine forms to match fashionable chests of drawers. Most had a straight top but some like this Sheraton example, right, could have more elaborate shaped crests and pediments.*

FIG 7.6: Purpose-made dressing tables *were available by the mid-18th century. Some had hinged flaps which were lifted to the back or sides revealing a mirror and drawers, as in this elegant example, while others were simple kneehole desks with a small pivoted toilet mirror positioned on top. By the 19th century larger pedestal-style dressing tables with mirrors were common.*

FIG 7.7: In the early 19th century *linen and clothes presses were available flanked by tall cupboards. This Regency example has a restrained appearance, with Egyptian touches in the finials and the tapered column mouldings down the sides. These pieces evolved into the more familiar wardrobe and separate chest of drawers in the Victorian period although clothes presses were still available.*

FIG 7.8: Four-poster beds *began to lose favour by the turn of the 19th century, and a range of bed types became popular in the Regency period. Half testers with a short canopy over the head of the bed were easier to manage and clean and remained popular during the 19th century as in this mid-Victorian example with distinctive curved corners on the cornice and richly carved footboard. Some beds had an equal-height head and footboard and were pushed up against a wall with light fabric draped over them from a wall-mounted feature. Another alternative had curtains hung from wooden or metal rails arranged in a variety of shapes above the bed. Day or sofa beds were also available (see FIG 2.23) in this period as the wealthy seemed obsessed with lounging around and sleeping.*

FIG 7.9: Washstands *became a standard fitting in the bedroom during the second half of the 18th century. Early types were often a simple tripod supporting a ceramic bowl with a stand on the stretchers below to hold a water jug. Sometimes these are called wig stands as they were convenient for powdering fashionable head pieces. More conventional desk types and corner washstands became popular during the late Georgian period, and Victorian versions often had marble tops and, by the late 19th century, a wooden splashback with glazed tiles, as in this example.*

FIG 7.10: By the mid-Victorian period, *furniture manufacturers were mass-producing bedroom furniture for the growing middle classes which was often sold as a suite including a large wardrobe, a dressing table, washstand, small bedside cupboards and chairs. The wardrobe could range from small pieces as in this example to grand tripartite versions with a range of drawers, and from the 1860s with a cheval mirror on the front (formerly they had been freestanding). Although tall hanging wardrobes were available from the early 19th century it was not until later in the century when the clothes hanger was invented that they became more common.*

FIG 7.11: Conventional beds *with just a head and footboard became more popular as the 19th century progressed. Many were polished or painted timber pieces with fashionable Gothic, Chippendale, Sheraton or Louis XV reproduction styles to match the other pieces in the bedroom suite. From the 1850s, brass beds became fashionable; cheaper versions were combined with enamelled iron typically in black or white, as in this example. Some brass beds had tall head posts which supported side rails so that wings of fabric could be draped down the sides imitating half testers.*

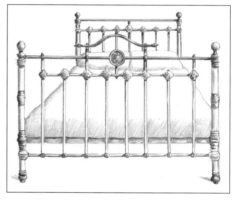

FIG 7.12: In the early 20th century, *the familiar bedroom suite including a hanging wardrobe, chest of drawers, dressing table, bedside cabinets and chairs was a popular purchase for middle class families moving into new suburban homes. Reproduction styles were still fashionable although the decoration was simplified and made cheaper by machine production, which began to influence furniture manufacturing from the 1880s. Art Deco breathed fresh air into contemporary bedrooms in the 1930s, with its curvaceous forms and stepped details shown here on this dressing table with a tripartite mirror and pedestal drawers.*

MISCELLANEOUS

Clocks, mirrors, trolleys, overmantels and screens

FIG 8.1: Longcase or grandfather clocks *are one of the most fascinating pieces of furniture with their beautifully decorated cases and intricate dials and workings. Their tall, thin form developed at first to house new longer weights in the middle of the 17th century. At this time the pendulum had a wide swing of up to 100 degrees but after the anchor escapement mechanism began to be adopted in the 1670s it was reduced to around 5 degrees. This meant longer pendulums could be used, which were more accurate and required less winding, and the longcase was ideal to house them. They were available in two variations: the 30-hour mechanism which needed winding once a day and the generally more expensive eight-day type which only needed to be wound once a week. The earliest examples often had ebonised cases, small 9" or 10" dials, and a flat top (left), while some of the finest William and Mary style pieces had lavish foliage marquetry cases*

and little cherubs in the corners (spandrels) around the clock face (centre). In the early 18th century the dial became gradually larger, around 11"-12" and by the 1730s often had an arched top to house additional features like the moon phases. Later Georgian examples had a shaped top often with three finials or urns and by the turn of the 19th century often featured Sheraton-style details (right). Longcase clocks remained popular until the end of the 19th century and displayed the Victorians' love for exuberant decoration (as a general rule clock makers were cautious and styles are often a few decades out of date).

FIG 8.2: Spices were a prized ingredient *to add much-needed flavour to dishes. From the mid-17th century, small spice cupboards were made specifically to store them with a series of small pull-out drawers behind a lockable hinged door. They were often decorated, as in this example from the late 17th century, with bold geometric patterns. Spice cupboards fell from favour in the early 19th century when spices began to be stored in metal tins.*

FIG 8.3: A whatnot or étagère *is a small shelving unit originally designed for books but which was used for all sorts of ornaments and knick-knacks by the Victorians. Early types from the late 18th century tend to be square in form with a series of shelves supported upon thin turned spindles. Whatnots were very popular in the 19th century when they were often quadrant shaped to fit into a corner, with graduated shelves, fancy decorative edging and busy spindles. Some had mirrored backs to reflect the object on the shelf and bamboo versions were also made when oriental furniture became popular in the 1870s.*

FIG 8.4: Georgian ladies *had to restrain their conversation while food was being served in case servants overheard their secrets. The problem was solved by furniture makers who in the 1730s developed a piece known in England as a dumbwaiter. This was a series of tiered round trays set upon a central shaft which allowed food and drink to be left next to the table so the servants could be dismissed ('dumb' referring to their silence). Georgian dumbwaiters were usually made of mahogany with a raised pie crust edge, as in this example, with three legs set upon castors so it could easily be moved around the room. Later Regency types were more varied in form some with rectangular shelves supported on pillars in the corners and gallery rails around the edge, while other woods and marble were also used for the trays. They only fell from fashion in the 1930s.*

FIG 8.5: Mirrors were a luxury product *before the Industrial Revolution. Venetian glass manufacturers had perfected the process of applying a silver reflective coating to the back of plate glass but their secrets were discovered by manufacturers in*

England by the second half of the 17th century. These early mirrors usually had a rectangular frame, some richly carved in the manner of Grinling Gibbons, others with fashionable marquetry, gilded or ebonised finishes (left). Some from the late 17th century had bolection moulded frames which had the thicker raised part of the moulding around the edge of the glass rather than the outer edge. Queen Anne types often had an arched top while mid-18th-century Rococo mirrors had lively sinuous and asymmetrical carving (centre). As glass could only be made in small sizes Rococo style foliage was used to cover up the joints between a series of sheets so they appeared as one large mirror. Oval-shaped mirrors were used in Adam-style interiors and small round concave mirrors were fashionable in the Regency period (right). Improved production of glass in the late 18th century and new techniques for making mirrors in the early Victorian period made them more affordable.

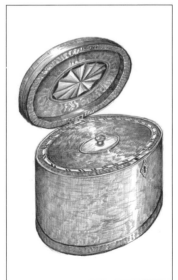

FIG 8.6: Although tea is considered England's national drink *it was only introduced into the country from China thanks to Charles II's Portuguese wife Catherine of Braganza after their wedding in 1662. Even in the mid-18th century it was expensive and restricted to specialist shops like apothecaries although smuggled tea was a cheaper option. It was around this time that wooden tea caddies were introduced, small wooden chests in which the metal canisters containing the tea, along with one for sugar, could be securely stored. In the late 18th century, oval and polygonal shapes were also popular with either one, two or three compartments within, and decorated with the fashionable Neoclassical motifs, as in this example. Small chest-shaped caddies were popular in the Regency period, often in the shape of a sarcophagus mounted on small brass animal feet. Victorian tea caddies were mass produced as tea was now imported from India as well as China, which helped lower the price until the late 19th century when pre-packed tea came on the market and they fell from use.*

FIG 8.7: Wine coolers became popular *in the homes of the wealthy from the early 18th century. Some were small tabletop pieces with a lead lining designed to hold a couple of bottles cooled by ice and water, others were larger bath types on legs and castors which could hold up to 50 bottles. Oval or round shapes were popular in earlier examples while Robert Adam designed some in a sarcophagus form, and late 18th-century examples feature Neoclassical motifs, as in this example.*

FIG 8.8: Another popular piece of furniture *in the 19th century was the Canterbury, an early form of magazine rack. It was named after a piece which was commissioned by the Archbishop of Canterbury to hold sheet music but was later used for all types of books or periodicals. A popular form in the first half of the 19th century had a row of shaped wooden stands, as in this example with the Prince of Wales plume of feathers in the centre. Victorian versions were more sturdy pieces, often in a rectangular form and with a rail around the top edge.*

FIG 8.9: Prior to the Second World War *all houses relied upon open fires for heating. There was very little control of the heat produced so fire screens which protect those sitting close to the flames were an essential piece of furniture. They also had the advantage that they could be used to cover the empty grate during summer so the blackened gaping hole was out of sight. Horse screens which had a single large panel supported on four legs (hence it looked like a horse) were common in the 18th and 19th century. The screen could be made from a variety of materials including wood, tapestry and even papier-mâché, and was usually decorated, as in this example with an Art Nouveau design. Late 18th century types were light and had small round or square panels. By the mid-19th century they tended to be more robust, heavy and richly decorated before more simple types became fashionable by the turn of the 20th century. Pole screens had a small panel or banner supported on a tall wooden pole, which were intended to be sited in the room close to the seated person rather than up close to the fire.*

**FIG 8.10:
Overmantels
were a decorative
timber structure**
*above the fireplace
surround or
chimneypiece. They
were fashionable
in Tudor and Stuart
homes with rich
carving in early
examples (top
left). They fell from
fashion in the late
17th century but
were revived by
the Victorians to
frame a mirror and
display ornaments
on shelves or little
cupboards (top
right). Later Arts and
Crafts types were
more restrained
(bottom left) and
could be extended to
the sides to include
seating and glass
display cupboards.
In the early 20th
century, oval mirrors
and plain pilasters*

imitating 18th century Classical styles were fashionable (bottom right).

Ince and Mayhew

William Ince and John Mayhew were two successful cabinet makers who went into partnership in 1759 and continued to produce high quality furniture until the latter's death in 1809. The pair published their *Universal System of Household Furniture* in parts between 1759-62, which included around 300 drawings intended to compete with Chippendale's Director. Their designs included Chinese, Gothic and Louis XV styles (many with fretwork decoration) and in addition to their own high quality pieces they were happy to produce pieces to the designs of others like Robert Adam.

REPRODUCTIONS AND FAKES

Dating furniture would be a much simpler process were it not for reproductions and fakes. Pieces have long been made to imitate a past style, especially in the 19th century. Many Victorians valued the association with historic periods like the Elizabethan or Queen Anne and felt secure buying a fine reproduction Chippendale piece. Furniture makers supplied them with their interpretations of old English and French pieces made in the manner of past masters. These perfectly legitimate pieces are often of high quality and have a value of their own.

There are many examples though of furniture which has been constructed or altered in some way that can fool the buyer. This was often done to repair, restore or modernise a piece with no intention to deceive. For instance, when tallboys fell from favour in the early 19th century it was common for them to be split and made into two small chests which would require some new work. In many cases these alterations were made with the intention of increasing the value of a piece. This age-old practice was generally done in one of three ways. A new piece was made in an old style and then cleverly distressed to make it look old. Alternatively, parts from more than one piece of furniture, especially tables, were married together to make a

completely new antique. Thirdly, it was common practice to make additions to a plain piece like adding inlays or carving parts into a fancier shape to increase its value. Although the finest fakery can fool all but the expert, there are some common tricks to look out for which should set a novice's alarm bells ringing when looking at a supposed antique.

The first aspect to study is the surface condition or patina of the piece. In the past, traditional methods of finishing a new piece was a lengthy process, which involved oiling the wood, treating it with beeswax and turpentine before carefully polishing it so that with the addition of time a piece should have a mellow or soft glow. Spirit based polishes were introduced in the 19th century and they create different results. For instance, they give mahogany its reddish tone so genuine Georgian examples should be a more golden colour. In order to simulate this patina on fake furniture, stains are used, so if you inspect an area which is not on show like underneath a table then signs of staining rather than a clean, slightly darkened wood indicate it could be a fake.

Although fakers have various clever techniques to distress furniture, some wear and tear from hundreds of years of use is hard to recreate. Look for a smooth, waxy finish where hands have rubbed the ends of the arms of chairs and touched the underside edge of tables over centuries of use. Feet would have rested upon the front stretcher of chairs so it should be worn but not down those along the sides and rear. Dirt and dust would have built up in patches across genuine pieces; if it is evenly distributed then it could be fake. Study any areas where parts can move or rub and check there are corresponding marks on the part they touch. Also be wary of sharp edges where you would expect to see them slightly rounded through use.

There can also be ways of identifying fakes through the materials used and the way the wood was worked. In general, wood was more plentiful in the past so original carving and turned patterns tend to be deeper and better proportioned, while modern reproductions will often have lighter frames. Fakers are usually trying to copy an exact piece so their tooling marks are precise whereas the original craftsman was only loosely following a design so could work freely and hence create little irregularities in his work. Veneers were hand-cut before machines took over the task in the second half of the 19th century, hence earlier sheets will be thicker, so be wary of veneers which appear wafer thin. Veneers were held in place by animal glues and after centuries of use will be expected to lift or crack around the edges, a perfect finish should be treated with suspicion. In general, glass was only available in small sheets before the 19th century, so should be set within glazing bars which were joined into the frames upon old cabinet or bookcase doors. If astragals are stuck onto one large sheet then it is a modern reproduction. Also check the interior and rear of carcasses for plywood and chipboard which only became mass-produced from the 1930s.

The way in which furniture has been constructed has changed over the centuries so, if possible, inspect the interior and underneath of a piece for little details which can indicate it is more modern than it appears. Always be wary if the finish of the wood does not match with its neighbouring part or if a length of carving or turned leg seems to end suddenly or part of the pattern is cut through which are signs that it has been made up from different pieces of furniture. Old chairs were fitted together using mortise and tenon joints; doweled joints and screwed corner blocks underneath tend to be Victorian or later. Metal screws were first introduced in the late 17th century and were handmade so the slit in the head will be roughly positioned. If they are dead centre or have a Phillips cross head then they are more modern. Old nails were square in profile; machine made round ones with a flat head only came into production in the late Victorian period. The shelves in old cabinets and bookcases were set into grooves down the sides; ones resting upon pegs or cleats were introduced in the 19th century. Check that the drawer boxes seem correct for the date. From the late 17th century they were fixed to the front using hand-cut dovetail joints; from the late 19th century these were machine-cut and will be more regular with thicker tails. The bottom of drawers in the 18th century were usually set in a rebate or held by the bearer underneath but in the early and mid-19th century they were restrained by a small beading around the inside edge. To check that handles are original (they are usually not) look on the inside of drawer fronts to see if there are other holes which show they have been changed at some point. Look for a slight dent and a different shade behind the ring or teardrop of a handle where it has hit the front and shaded it from the sun over the centuries. The bun feet of large pieces of old furniture were often replaced by bracket types to suit fashion or through wear and tear; if the piece is original then the single hole from the earlier foot should still be visible.

These tips can be a starting point to help date furniture and spot fakes. However, certain details like the correct proportions of a piece, the patina of the surface or the tooling marks on carving can only be recognised if you have a good knowledge of the originals. Therefore, anyone who would like to become more of an expert in the field should study furniture in country houses, museums and reputable antique dealers which is likely to have been authenticated by experts. A good starting point is the collection in two particular museums: The Victoria and Albert Museum in London (www.vam.ac.uk) and Temple Newsam House in Leeds (www. leeds.gov.uk/museumsandgalleries/ templenewsamhouse).

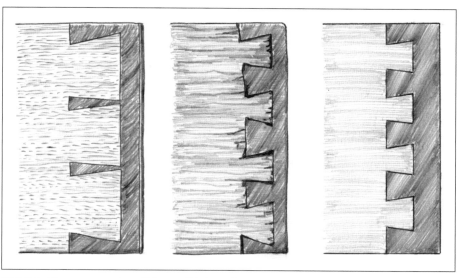

FIG 9.1: These examples of dovetail joints *show how attaching the drawer front to the sides varied over the centuries. The finest Georgian pieces of furniture typically had thin, hand-cut dovetails (left), while this hand-cut Victorian example (centre) is typically of lesser quality work. Machine-cut joints were regular and evenly spaced out with sharp edges (right) and became widespread from the late 19th century.*

GLOSSARY

Acanthus: A thick, leafy plant which was a popular Classical decorative form.

Anthemion: A honeysuckle leaf and flower design.

Apron: A plain or shaped piece of timber fixed below the top of tables, desks and under the seat of some chairs.

Arabesque: A pattern of foliated scrolls.

Architrave: The moulded surround of a cupboard or door opening.

Armoire: A French style of wardrobe.

Astragals: A thin wooden moulding used for glazing bars on glass doors.

Ball-and-Claw: A wooden foot shaped like an animal's talons grasping a ball.

Balusters: Individual turned supports usually found on the backs of chairs or up the sides of stairs.

Banding/Cross banding: A decorative border around a piece of furniture. Cross banding is where the grain of the strip is at right angles to the outer edge.

Baroque: A Classical style with massive scale, deep features and rich ornamentation.

Beading: A thin, semicircular moulding strip.

Bevel: An edge that has been cut at an angle.

Bolection: An ogee-shaped moulding around an opening with the raised part closest to the centre.

Bombe: A swollen, curved form.

Boulle/Buhl: Marquetry with tortoiseshell or brass, forming elaborate designs often set in ebony perfected by André Charles Boulle.

Bracket foot: A foot used on chests and cabinets which has a straight outer edge and curved inner.

Breakfront: The central section of a piece of furniture which projects forward.

Bun/ball foot: A round foot used on early chests and cabinets. A bun is a flatter version of the ball.

Burr: The curly or circular patterns formed in the grain of certain woods like walnut.

Cabriole leg: A double-curved leg which projects outwards at the top (knee) and then tapers down in an 's' shape to the foot.

Canted: A surface like the corners of some chests of drawers set at an angle.

Capital: The decorated top of a column.

Carcass: The body of a chest or cabinet onto which veneers were applied.

Caryatids: Female figures supporting an entablature.

Castor: A small wheel held in a metal bracket under the foot of portable furniture.

Cellaret: An 18th century portable chest or cabinet for bottles and glasses.

Chaise longue: A long upholstered chair with a sloping back for relaxing.

Classical order: A style of Classical architecture which is most easily recognised by the style of the capital used on the columns.

Chiffonier: A French word for a small sideboard.

Chinoiserie: A French term for Chinese design and influence.

Cockbeading: A thin round beading around the edges of drawers.

Commode: An elaborately decorated low chest of drawers or cupboard.

Concave: Inward curving surface.

Console table: A small, often decorative, table which was fixed to the wall.

Convex: Outward curving surface.

Console: An ornamental bracket.

Cornice: A plain or decorative moulding around the top of a wall.

Credenza: An elaborate 19th century sideboard usually with a mirrored back.

Cresting: A decorative carved piece of wood on top of a cabinet or mirror.

Cusp: A pointed junction between two curves which form a 'v' shape. Found in medieval window tracery.

Damask: Originally a silk fabric from Damascus but now generally applied to a distinctive pattern of two-dimensional stylised foliage.

Dentil: A thin moulding comprising a row of raised and sunken square blocks.

Dovetail: A joint made of wedge-shaped projections and sockets.

Dowel: A headless wooden pin which fits into a corresponding hole on another piece.

Drop leaf: An extension to a table which drops to the side when not in use.

Ebonise: To apply a black stain to wood to simulate ebony.

Egg and dart: A decorative moulding with an egg shape divided up by the pointed end of a dart.

Entablature: The horizontal upper feature supported by columns in an Ancient temple.

Escutcheon: A metal ring or plate metal around a keyhole.

Fall front: A front panel on a bureau or desk which forms a writing surface when lowered down.

Fleur-de-lis: A stylised iris flower design.

Figured curl: Wood with a swirling pattern.

Finial: A vertical carved or turned feature which sits at the end of the ridge of a roof usually above a gable end.

Fluted: A column, pilaster or leg with narrow concave grooves running vertically up it.

Fretwork: A geometric grid of interlacing lines formed into a band or panel.

Frieze: A horizontal ornamental border.

Gallery: A short ornamental railing around the top of a piece of furniture.

Gadrooning: A row of short vertical or diagonal raised convex flutes or bands.

Gate-leg table: A round or oval table with flaps which are raised up on framed supports which swing out from underneath the central section.

Gesso: A mix of size and gypsum paste which could be incised or raised up to imitate carved wood.

Gilding: Gold leaf applied to a surface.

Herringbone: A pattern formed from short, angled pieces which appear like a horizontal zigzag. Used in brickwork, masonry and parquet flooring.

Inlay: A pattern made out of thin layers of wood and other materials set in depressions formed in solid wood furniture.

Japanning: Methods using resins and paint to imitate lacquered furniture from the Far East.

Knee: The projecting top of a cabriole leg.

Lacquer: A high gloss oriental varnish.

Laminated wood/Plywood: A board made from thin sheets of wood bonded together with the grain in opposite directions to make a strong and stable material used in furniture.

Linenfold: A form of panelling popular in the early Tudor period which looks like rippled or folded fabric.

Marquetry: Patterns formed in the veneered surface of furniture from contrasting wood and other materials.

Mortise and tenon: A joint formed from a projecting tongue (tenon) which fits into a similar sized hole (mortise) in another part, held in place by pegs.

Moulding: An ornamental strip of wood with a decorative profile formed from concave, convex and angled elements.

Muntin: A vertical member between two panels.

Neoclassical: The new style of classical design from the late 18th century which used forms direct from Ancient

Roman, Etruscan and Greek. Previous Classical styles had been based upon the work of Renaissance architects.

Orders: The different styles and proportions of the plinth, column and entablature from Classical architecture.

Ormolu: Gilded bronze or brass decorative mounts which were popular on late 18th and early 19th century furniture.

Palmette: A stylised palm leaf motif.

Panel: A rectangular or square piece of wood set within a frame. A fielded panel has a raised central section with chamfered sides.

Parquetry: A geometric design formed from pieces of inlaid wood.

Patera: A round or oval motif based upon a patera which was a shallow Roman dish.

Patina: A term used to describe the sheen formed on the surface of furniture due to wear and age.

Pedestal: An upright support. In furniture it can be either a turned central pillar on a round table or a set of drawers at either end of a desk.

Pediment: A low pitched triangular feature found on the top of cabinets and bookcases. A broken pediment has a gap in the centre.

Pendant: A hanging carved feature.

Pie crust: The thin raised edge around a small table or dumb waiter which looks like the crust around a pie.

Pilaster: A flat column projecting slightly from the wall.

Plinth: A low, slightly projecting base around the foot of large pieces of furniture.

Rail: A horizontal piece of timber.

Reeding: Thin, vertical convex lines on pilasters and legs, popular in the Regency period (opposite of fluting).

Renaissance: A rebirth of art, literature and learning based upon that of the Classical world across Europe from the 14th century. Its effects were not to be influential in Britain until the 16th century.

Rococo: An asymmetrical and florid style of the mid-18th century full of swirls, scrolls and shells, applied to plaster work, carving and furniture and often in white and gold.

Romayne work: Decorative medallions or panels with the side profile of a human head, popular in the 16th and early 17th century.

Sarcophagus: A coffin-shaped box with tapering sides.

Scroll: An ornamental motif based on the end of a rolled-up piece of paper or scroll.

Segmental arch: A bow-shaped arch which is formed from a segment of a larger arch.

Serpentine: In furniture an S-shaped, curved form usually on the front of chests and cabinets.

Splat: A flat, vertical piece of wood up the centre of the back of a chair.

Stile: A vertical piece of timber which forms the side of frames and panels.

Strapwork: A raised, flat decoration formed into lozenges and other geometric shapes which was popular on panelling and other carving in late 16th and early 17th centuries.

Stringing: Very narrow bands of wooden or brass inlaid in wood.

Stretcher: A horizontal timber member connecting the legs of chairs and tables.

Swag: An ornamental carving which looks like fabric or garlands draped between two points.

Swan neck: An 's' shape like the neck of a swan.

Tester: Another word for the canopy above a four-poster bed.

Turned: A rounded block of wood carved by rotating it while cutting a profile into it with a tool.

Veneer: Thin sheets of fine wood applied to a timber base.

Whatnot: A small stand with a series of shelves used for books or display ornaments.